Everyday 3-D Shapes

Pyramids

by Laura Hamilton Waxman
illustrated by Kathryn Mitter

Content Consultant: Paula J. Maida, PhD,
Department of Mathematics, Western Connecticut State University

magic
wagon

visit us at
www.abdopublishing.com

Published by Magic Wagon, a division of the ABDO Group, PO Box 398166, Minneapolis, MN 55439. Copyright © 2013 by Abdo Consulting Group, Inc. International copyrights reserved in all countries. All rights reserved. No part of this book may be reproduced in any form without written permission from the publisher.

Looking Glass Library™ is a trademark and logo of Magic Wagon. Printed in the United States of America, North Mankato, Minnesota.
042012
092012

 THIS BOOK CONTAINS AT LEAST 10% RECYCLED MATERIALS.

Text by Laura Hamilton Waxman
Illustrations by Kathryn Mitter
Edited by Rebecca Felix
Series design by Craig Hinton

Library of Congress Cataloging-in-Publication Data
Waxman, Laura Hamilton.
Pyramids / by Laura Hamilton Waxman ; illustrated by Kathryn Mitter.
pages cm -- (Everyday 3-D Shapes)
Content Consultant: Dr. Paula Maida.
ISBN 978-1-61641-876-2
1. Pyramid (Geometry)--Juvenile literature. 2. Shapes--Juvenile literature. 3. Geometry, Solid--Juvenile literature. I. Mitter, Kathy, illustrator. II. Title.
QA491.W3783 2012
516'.156--dc23
2012007119

Pyramids have a point on top.

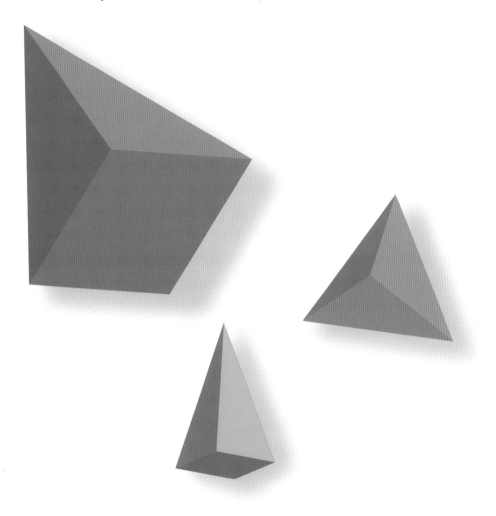

A flat bottom is where they stop.

Triangles make each leaning face.

Faces stretch out wide at the base.

Look around for this shape's look.

Search for pyramids in this book.

FARM FRESH

SALSA

JAM

6

8

Ben sees bright stacks of fruit to eat.

Built like pyramids, nice and neat.

Pyramid roofs block rain and snow.

They stay attached as strong winds blow.

Jill peeks through this pyramid's door.

She finds toys camping on its floor.

Ben spots pyramids with burning tips.

Each changes shape as it melts and drips.

15

This glass pyramid weighs a lot.

It helps keep papers in one spot.

Jill climbs this pyramid in a crawl.

The pyramid top gets very small!

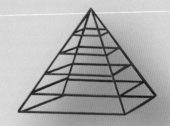

19

Ben's project is on stars and space.

He wins the trophy for first place!

Pyramids aren't just in this book.

They're all around you. Take a look!

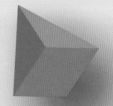

I Spy a Pyramid Game

Look around. Find a pyramid. Then say, "I spy a pyramid that is . . ." and name its color. Everyone has to guess what pyramid you see. Then it is someone else's turn to spy a pyramid. You can guess what it is.

Count the Pyramids Game

Choose a room in your home. Count how many pyramids you can find.

Glossary

base: the bottom of something.

pyramid: a shape with a flat base and triangle faces that meet together at a single point.

shape: the form or look something has.

triangle: a shape with three straight sides and three corners.